MW00356379

TO:

_____

FROM:

_____

DATE:

_____

© 2020 Christian Art Gifts, RSA
Christian Art Gifts Inc., IL, USA
Printed in Vietnam

DELIGHT YOURSELF IN THE LORD, AND HE WILL
GIVE YOU THE DESIRES OF YOUR HEART. PS. 37:4

THE LORD IS MY LIGHT AND MY SALVATION—WHOM SHALL I FEAR? THE
LORD IS THE STRONGHOLD OF MY LIFE—OF WHOM SHALL I BE AFRAID?

PS. 27:1

THE LORD HIMSELF GOES BEFORE YOU AND WILL BE WITH YOU;
HE WILL NEVER LEAVE YOU NOR FORSAKE YOU. DEUT. 31:8

GOD IS WORKING IN YOU, GIVING YOU THE DESIRE TO
OBEY HIM AND THE POWER TO DO WHAT PLEASES HIM.
PHIL. 2:13

I CAN DO EVERYTHING THROUGH CHRIST,
WHO GIVES ME STRENGTH. PHIL. 4:13

IF YOU WANT TO KNOW WHAT GOD WANTS YOU TO DO,
ASK HIM, AND HE WILL GLADLY TELL YOU. JAMES 1:5

CREATE IN ME A PURE HEART, O GOD, AND RENEW
A STEADFAST SPIRIT WITHIN ME. PS. 51:10

IF ANYONE IS IN CHRIST, HE IS A NEW CREATION;
THE OLD HAS GONE, THE NEW HAS COME! 2 COR. 5:17

CAST YOUR CARES ON THE LORD AND HE WILL SUSTAIN YOU.

PS. 55:22

THE LORD YOUR GOD IS WITH YOU, HE IS MIGHTY TO SAVE. HE WILL
TAKE GREAT DELIGHT IN YOU, HE WILL QUIET YOU WITH HIS LOVE.
ZEPH. 3:17

THE LORD IS FAITHFUL TO ALL HIS PROMISES
AND LOVING TOWARD ALL HE HAS MADE. PS. 145:13

IN YOU, O LORD, DO I PUT MY TRUST. PS. 71:1

"BE STRONG AND COURAGEOUS . . . THE LORD YOUR GOD
WILL BE WITH YOU WHEREVER YOU GO." JOSH. 1:9

DEPEND ON THE LORD IN WHATEVER YOU DO,
AND YOUR PLANS WILL SUCCEED. PROV. 16:3

SINCE WE HAVE BEEN JUSTIFIED THROUGH FAITH, WE HAVE PEACE
WITH GOD THROUGH OUR LORD JESUS CHRIST. ROM. 5:1

THE LORD IS MY ROCK, MY FORTRESS AND MY DELIVERER;
MY GOD IS MY ROCK, IN WHOM I TAKE REFUGE. PS. 18:2

"IF ANYONE WOULD COME AFTER ME, HE MUST DENY HIMSELF
AND TAKE UP HIS CROSS AND FOLLOW ME." MATT. 16:24

THE WORD OF THE LORD IS RIGHT AND TRUE;
HE IS FAITHFUL IN ALL HE DOES. PS. 33:4

THE LORD IS MY STRENGTH, MY SHIELD FROM EVERY DANGER.
I TRUST IN HIM WITH ALL MY HEART. PS. 28:7

IN HIM WE HAVE REDEMPTION THROUGH HIS BLOOD,
THE FORGIVENESS OF SINS, IN ACCORDANCE WITH
THE RICHES OF GOD'S GRACE. EPH. 1:7

I TRUST IN YOUR UNFAILING LOVE. I WILL REJOICE
BECAUSE YOU HAVE RESCUED ME. PS. 13:5

LIVE A LIFE OF LOVE, JUST AS CHRIST LOVED US
AND GAVE HIMSELF UP FOR US. EPH. 5:2

"YOU WILL CALL UPON ME AND COME AND PRAY TO ME, AND I WILL
LISTEN TO YOU. YOU WILL SEEK ME AND FIND ME WHEN YOU SEEK
ME WITH ALL YOUR HEART." JER. 29:12-13

MY SOUL FINDS REST IN GOD ALONE;
MY SALVATION COMES FROM HIM. PS. 62:1

DELIGHT YOURSELF IN THE LORD, AND HE WILL
GIVE YOU THE DESIRES OF YOUR HEART. PS. 37:4

THE LORD IS MY LIGHT AND MY SALVATION—WHOM SHALL I FEAR? THE
LORD IS THE STRONGHOLD OF MY LIFE—OF WHOM SHALL I BE AFRAID?

PS. 27:1

THE LORD HIMSELF GOES BEFORE YOU AND WILL BE WITH YOU;
HE WILL NEVER LEAVE YOU NOR FORSAKE YOU. DEUT. 31:8

GOD IS WORKING IN YOU, GIVING YOU THE DESIRE TO
OBEY HIM AND THE POWER TO DO WHAT PLEASES HIM.
PHIL. 2:13

I CAN DO EVERYTHING THROUGH CHRIST,
WHO GIVES ME STRENGTH. PHIL. 4:13

IF YOU WANT TO KNOW WHAT GOD WANTS YOU TO DO,
ASK HIM, AND HE WILL GLADLY TELL YOU. JAMES 1:5

CREATE IN ME A PURE HEART, O GOD, AND RENEW
A STEADFAST SPIRIT WITHIN ME. PS. 51:10

IF ANYONE IS IN CHRIST, HE IS A NEW CREATION;
THE OLD HAS GONE, THE NEW HAS COME! 2 COR. 5:17

CAST YOUR CARES ON THE LORD AND HE WILL SUSTAIN YOU.

PS. 55:22

THE LORD YOUR GOD IS WITH YOU, HE IS MIGHTY TO SAVE. HE WILL
TAKE GREAT DELIGHT IN YOU, HE WILL QUIET YOU WITH HIS LOVE.
ZEPH. 3:17

THE LORD IS FAITHFUL TO ALL HIS PROMISES
AND LOVING TOWARD ALL HE HAS MADE. PS. 145:13

IN YOU, O LORD, DO I PUT MY TRUST. PS. 71:1

"BE STRONG AND COURAGEOUS . . . THE LORD YOUR GOD
WILL BE WITH YOU WHEREVER YOU GO." JOSH. 1:9

DEPEND ON THE LORD IN WHATEVER YOU DO,
AND YOUR PLANS WILL SUCCEED. PROV. 16:3

SINCE WE HAVE BEEN JUSTIFIED THROUGH FAITH, WE HAVE PEACE
WITH GOD THROUGH OUR LORD JESUS CHRIST. ROM. 5:1

THE LORD IS MY ROCK, MY FORTRESS AND MY DELIVERER;
MY GOD IS MY ROCK, IN WHOM I TAKE REFUGE. PS. 18:2

"IF ANYONE WOULD COME AFTER ME, HE MUST DENY HIMSELF
AND TAKE UP HIS CROSS AND FOLLOW ME." MATT. 16:24

THE WORD OF THE LORD IS RIGHT AND TRUE;
HE IS FAITHFUL IN ALL HE DOES. PS. 33:4

THE LORD IS MY STRENGTH, MY SHIELD FROM EVERY DANGER.
I TRUST IN HIM WITH ALL MY HEART. PS. 28:7

IN HIM WE HAVE REDEMPTION THROUGH HIS BLOOD,
THE FORGIVENESS OF SINS, IN ACCORDANCE WITH
THE RICHES OF GOD'S GRACE. EPH. 1:7

I TRUST IN YOUR UNFAILING LOVE. I WILL REJOICE

BECAUSE YOU HAVE RESCUED ME. PS. 13:5

LIVE A LIFE OF LOVE, JUST AS CHRIST LOVED US
AND GAVE HIMSELF UP FOR US. EPH. 5:2

"YOU WILL CALL UPON ME AND COME AND PRAY TO ME, AND I WILL
LISTEN TO YOU. YOU WILL SEEK ME AND FIND ME WHEN YOU SEEK
ME WITH ALL YOUR HEART." JER. 29:12-13

MY SOUL FINDS REST IN GOD ALONE;
MY SALVATION COMES FROM HIM. PS. 62:1

DELIGHT YOURSELF IN THE LORD, AND HE WILL
GIVE YOU THE DESIRES OF YOUR HEART. PS. 37:4

THE LORD IS MY LIGHT AND MY SALVATION—WHOM SHALL I FEAR? THE
LORD IS THE STRONGHOLD OF MY LIFE—OF WHOM SHALL I BE AFRAID?

PS. 27:1

THE LORD HIMSELF GOES BEFORE YOU AND WILL BE WITH YOU;
HE WILL NEVER LEAVE YOU NOR FORSAKE YOU. DEUT. 31:8

GOD IS WORKING IN YOU, GIVING YOU THE DESIRE TO
OBEY HIM AND THE POWER TO DO WHAT PLEASES HIM.
PHIL. 2:13

I CAN DO EVERYTHING THROUGH CHRIST,
WHO GIVES ME STRENGTH. PHIL. 4:13

IF YOU WANT TO KNOW WHAT GOD WANTS YOU TO DO,
ASK HIM, AND HE WILL GLADLY TELL YOU. JAMES 1:5

CREATE IN ME A PURE HEART, O GOD, AND RENEW
A STEADFAST SPIRIT WITHIN ME. PS. 51:10

IF ANYONE IS IN CHRIST, HE IS A NEW CREATION;
THE OLD HAS GONE, THE NEW HAS COME! 2 COR. 5:17

CAST YOUR CARES ON THE LORD AND HE WILL SUSTAIN YOU.

PS. 55:22

THE LORD YOUR GOD IS WITH YOU, HE IS MIGHTY TO SAVE. HE WILL
TAKE GREAT DELIGHT IN YOU, HE WILL QUIET YOU WITH HIS LOVE.
ZEPH. 3:17

THE LORD IS FAITHFUL TO ALL HIS PROMISES
AND LOVING TOWARD ALL HE HAS MADE. PS. 145:13

IN YOU, O LORD, DO I PUT MY TRUST. PS. 71:1

"BE STRONG AND COURAGEOUS . . . THE LORD YOUR GOD
WILL BE WITH YOU WHEREVER YOU GO." JOSH. 1:9

DEPEND ON THE LORD IN WHATEVER YOU DO,
AND YOUR PLANS WILL SUCCEED. PROV. 16:3

SINCE WE HAVE BEEN JUSTIFIED THROUGH FAITH, WE HAVE PEACE
WITH GOD THROUGH OUR LORD JESUS CHRIST. ROM. 5:1

THE LORD IS MY ROCK, MY FORTRESS AND MY DELIVERER;
MY GOD IS MY ROCK, IN WHOM I TAKE REFUGE. PS. 18:2

"IF ANYONE WOULD COME AFTER ME, HE MUST DENY HIMSELF
AND TAKE UP HIS CROSS AND FOLLOW ME." MATT. 16:24

THE WORD OF THE LORD IS RIGHT AND TRUE;
HE IS FAITHFUL IN ALL HE DOES. PS. 33:4

THE LORD IS MY STRENGTH, MY SHIELD FROM EVERY DANGER.
I TRUST IN HIM WITH ALL MY HEART. PS. 28:7

IN HIM WE HAVE REDEMPTION THROUGH HIS BLOOD,
THE FORGIVENESS OF SINS, IN ACCORDANCE WITH
THE RICHES OF GOD'S GRACE. EPH. 1:7

I TRUST IN YOUR UNFAILING LOVE. I WILL REJOICE
BECAUSE YOU HAVE RESCUED ME. PS. 13:5

LIVE A LIFE OF LOVE, JUST AS CHRIST LOVED US
AND GAVE HIMSELF UP FOR US. EPH. 5:2

"YOU WILL CALL UPON ME AND COME AND PRAY TO ME, AND I WILL
LISTEN TO YOU. YOU WILL SEEK ME AND FIND ME WHEN YOU SEEK
ME WITH ALL YOUR HEART." JER. 29:12-13

MY SOUL FINDS REST IN GOD ALONE;
MY SALVATION COMES FROM HIM. PS. 62:1

DELIGHT YOURSELF IN THE LORD, AND HE WILL
GIVE YOU THE DESIRES OF YOUR HEART. PS. 37:4

THE LORD IS MY LIGHT AND MY SALVATION—WHOM SHALL I FEAR? THE
LORD IS THE STRONGHOLD OF MY LIFE—OF WHOM SHALL I BE AFRAID?
PS. 27:1

THE LORD HIMSELF GOES BEFORE YOU AND WILL BE WITH YOU;
HE WILL NEVER LEAVE YOU NOR FORSAKE YOU. DEUT. 31:8

GOD IS WORKING IN YOU, GIVING YOU THE DESIRE TO
OBEY HIM AND THE POWER TO DO WHAT PLEASES HIM.
PHIL. 2:13

I CAN DO EVERYTHING THROUGH CHRIST,
WHO GIVES ME STRENGTH. PHIL. 4:13

IF YOU WANT TO KNOW WHAT GOD WANTS YOU TO DO,
ASK HIM, AND HE WILL GLADLY TELL YOU. JAMES 1:5

CREATE IN ME A PURE HEART, O GOD, AND RENEW
A STEADFAST SPIRIT WITHIN ME. PS. 51:10

IF ANYONE IS IN CHRIST, HE IS A NEW CREATION;
THE OLD HAS GONE, THE NEW HAS COME! 2 COR. 5:17

CAST YOUR CARES ON THE LORD AND HE WILL SUSTAIN YOU.

PS. 55:22

THE LORD YOUR GOD IS WITH YOU, HE IS MIGHTY TO SAVE. HE WILL
TAKE GREAT DELIGHT IN YOU, HE WILL QUIET YOU WITH HIS LOVE.
ZEPH. 3:17

THE LORD IS FAITHFUL TO ALL HIS PROMISES
AND LOVING TOWARD ALL HE HAS MADE. PS. 145:13

IN YOU, O LORD, DO I PUT MY TRUST. PS. 71:1

"BE STRONG AND COURAGEOUS . . . THE LORD YOUR GOD
WILL BE WITH YOU WHEREVER YOU GO." JOSH. 1:9

DEPEND ON THE LORD IN WHATEVER YOU DO,
AND YOUR PLANS WILL SUCCEED. PROV. 16:3

SINCE WE HAVE BEEN JUSTIFIED THROUGH FAITH, WE HAVE PEACE
WITH GOD THROUGH OUR LORD JESUS CHRIST. ROM. 5:1

THE LORD IS MY ROCK, MY FORTRESS AND MY DELIVERER;
MY GOD IS MY ROCK, IN WHOM I TAKE REFUGE. PS. 18:2

"IF ANYONE WOULD COME AFTER ME, HE MUST DENY HIMSELF
AND TAKE UP HIS CROSS AND FOLLOW ME." MATT. 16:24

THE WORD OF THE LORD IS RIGHT AND TRUE;
HE IS FAITHFUL IN ALL HE DOES. PS. 33:4

THE LORD IS MY STRENGTH, MY SHIELD FROM EVERY DANGER.
I TRUST IN HIM WITH ALL MY HEART. PS. 28:7

IN HIM WE HAVE REDEMPTION THROUGH HIS BLOOD,
THE FORGIVENESS OF SINS, IN ACCORDANCE WITH
THE RICHES OF GOD'S GRACE. EPH. 1:7

I TRUST IN YOUR UNFAILING LOVE. I WILL REJOICE
BECAUSE YOU HAVE RESCUED ME. PS. 13:5

LIVE A LIFE OF LOVE, JUST AS CHRIST LOVED US
AND GAVE HIMSELF UP FOR US. EPH. 5:2

"YOU WILL CALL UPON ME AND COME AND PRAY TO ME, AND I WILL
LISTEN TO YOU. YOU WILL SEEK ME AND FIND ME WHEN YOU SEEK
ME WITH ALL YOUR HEART." JER. 29:12-13

MY SOUL FINDS REST IN GOD ALONE;
MY SALVATION COMES FROM HIM. PS. 62:1

DELIGHT YOURSELF IN THE LORD, AND HE WILL
GIVE YOU THE DESIRES OF YOUR HEART. PS. 37:4

THE LORD IS MY LIGHT AND MY SALVATION—WHOM SHALL I FEAR? THE
LORD IS THE STRONGHOLD OF MY LIFE—OF WHOM SHALL I BE AFRAID?

PS. 27:1

THE LORD HIMSELF GOES BEFORE YOU AND WILL BE WITH YOU;
HE WILL NEVER LEAVE YOU NOR FORSAKE YOU. DEUT. 31:8

GOD IS WORKING IN YOU, GIVING YOU THE DESIRE TO
OBEY HIM AND THE POWER TO DO WHAT PLEASES HIM.
PHIL. 2:13

I CAN DO EVERYTHING THROUGH CHRIST,
WHO GIVES ME STRENGTH. PHIL. 4:13

IF YOU WANT TO KNOW WHAT GOD WANTS YOU TO DO,
ASK HIM, AND HE WILL GLADLY TELL YOU. JAMES 1:5

CREATE IN ME A PURE HEART, O GOD, AND RENEW
A STEADFAST SPIRIT WITHIN ME. PS. 51:10

IF ANYONE IS IN CHRIST, HE IS A NEW CREATION;
THE OLD HAS GONE, THE NEW HAS COME! 2 COR. 5:17

CAST YOUR CARES ON THE LORD AND HE WILL SUSTAIN YOU.

PS. 55:22

THE LORD YOUR GOD IS WITH YOU, HE IS MIGHTY TO SAVE. HE WILL
TAKE GREAT DELIGHT IN YOU, HE WILL QUIET YOU WITH HIS LOVE.
ZEPH. 3:17

THE LORD IS FAITHFUL TO ALL HIS PROMISES
AND LOVING TOWARD ALL HE HAS MADE. PS. 145:13

IN YOU, O LORD, DO I PUT MY TRUST. PS. 71:1

"BE STRONG AND COURAGEOUS . . . THE LORD YOUR GOD
WILL BE WITH YOU WHEREVER YOU GO." JOSH. 1:9

DEPEND ON THE LORD IN WHATEVER YOU DO,
AND YOUR PLANS WILL SUCCEED. PROV. 16:3

SINCE WE HAVE BEEN JUSTIFIED THROUGH FAITH, WE HAVE PEACE
WITH GOD THROUGH OUR LORD JESUS CHRIST. ROM. 5:1

THE LORD IS MY ROCK, MY FORTRESS AND MY DELIVERER;
MY GOD IS MY ROCK, IN WHOM I TAKE REFUGE. PS. 18:2

"IF ANYONE WOULD COME AFTER ME, HE MUST DENY HIMSELF
AND TAKE UP HIS CROSS AND FOLLOW ME." MATT. 16:24

THE WORD OF THE LORD IS RIGHT AND TRUE;
HE IS FAITHFUL IN ALL HE DOES. PS. 33:4

THE LORD IS MY STRENGTH, MY SHIELD FROM EVERY DANGER.
I TRUST IN HIM WITH ALL MY HEART. PS. 28:7

IN HIM WE HAVE REDEMPTION THROUGH HIS BLOOD,
THE FORGIVENESS OF SINS, IN ACCORDANCE WITH
THE RICHES OF GOD'S GRACE. EPH. 1:7

I TRUST IN YOUR UNFAILING LOVE. I WILL REJOICE
BECAUSE YOU HAVE RESCUED ME. PS. 13:5

LIVE A LIFE OF LOVE, JUST AS CHRIST LOVED US
AND GAVE HIMSELF UP FOR US. EPH. 5:2

"YOU WILL CALL UPON ME AND COME AND PRAY TO ME, AND I WILL
LISTEN TO YOU. YOU WILL SEEK ME AND FIND ME WHEN YOU SEEK
ME WITH ALL YOUR HEART." JER. 29:12-13

MY SOUL FINDS REST IN GOD ALONE;
MY SALVATION COMES FROM HIM. PS. 62:1

DELIGHT YOURSELF IN THE LORD, AND HE WILL
GIVE YOU THE DESIRES OF YOUR HEART. PS. 37:4

THE LORD IS MY LIGHT AND MY SALVATION—WHOM SHALL I FEAR? THE
LORD IS THE STRONGHOLD OF MY LIFE—OF WHOM SHALL I BE AFRAID?

PS. 27:1

THE LORD HIMSELF GOES BEFORE YOU AND WILL BE WITH YOU;
HE WILL NEVER LEAVE YOU NOR FORSAKE YOU. DEUT. 31:8

GOD IS WORKING IN YOU, GIVING YOU THE DESIRE TO
OBEY HIM AND THE POWER TO DO WHAT PLEASES HIM.
PHIL. 2:13

I CAN DO EVERYTHING THROUGH CHRIST,
WHO GIVES ME STRENGTH. PHIL. 4:13

_____

_____

_____

_____

_____

_____

_____

_____

_____

_____

_____

_____

_____

_____

_____

_____

_____

_____

_____

_____

_____

IF YOU WANT TO KNOW WHAT GOD WANTS YOU TO DO,
ASK HIM, AND HE WILL GLADLY TELL YOU. JAMES 1:5

CREATE IN ME A PURE HEART, O GOD, AND RENEW
A STEADFAST SPIRIT WITHIN ME. PS. 51:10

IF ANYONE IS IN CHRIST, HE IS A NEW CREATION;
THE OLD HAS GONE, THE NEW HAS COME! 2 COR. 5:17

CAST YOUR CARES ON THE LORD AND HE WILL SUSTAIN YOU.

PS. 55:22

THE LORD YOUR GOD IS WITH YOU, HE IS MIGHTY TO SAVE. HE WILL
TAKE GREAT DELIGHT IN YOU, HE WILL QUIET YOU WITH HIS LOVE.
ZEPH. 3:17

THE LORD IS FAITHFUL TO ALL HIS PROMISES
AND LOVING TOWARD ALL HE HAS MADE. PS. 145:13

IN YOU, O LORD, DO I PUT MY TRUST. PS. 71:1

"BE STRONG AND COURAGEOUS . . . THE LORD YOUR GOD
WILL BE WITH YOU WHEREVER YOU GO." JOSH. 1:9

DEPEND ON THE LORD IN WHATEVER YOU DO,
AND YOUR PLANS WILL SUCCEED. PROV. 16:3

SINCE WE HAVE BEEN JUSTIFIED THROUGH FAITH, WE HAVE PEACE
WITH GOD THROUGH OUR LORD JESUS CHRIST. ROM. 5:1

THE LORD IS MY ROCK, MY FORTRESS AND MY DELIVERER;
MY GOD IS MY ROCK, IN WHOM I TAKE REFUGE. PS. 18:2

_____

_____

_____

_____

_____

_____

_____

_____

_____

_____

_____

_____

_____

_____

_____

_____

_____

_____

_____

_____

_____

_____

_____

_____

"IF ANYONE WOULD COME AFTER ME, HE MUST DENY HIMSELF
AND TAKE UP HIS CROSS AND FOLLOW ME." MATT. 16:24

THE WORD OF THE LORD IS RIGHT AND TRUE;
HE IS FAITHFUL IN ALL HE DOES. PS. 33:4

THE LORD IS MY STRENGTH, MY SHIELD FROM EVERY DANGER.
I TRUST IN HIM WITH ALL MY HEART. PS. 28:7

IN HIM WE HAVE REDEMPTION THROUGH HIS BLOOD,
THE FORGIVENESS OF SINS, IN ACCORDANCE WITH
THE RICHES OF GOD'S GRACE. EPH. 1:7

I TRUST IN YOUR UNFAILING LOVE. I WILL REJOICE
BECAUSE YOU HAVE RESCUED ME. PS. 13:5

LIVE A LIFE OF LOVE, JUST AS CHRIST LOVED US
AND GAVE HIMSELF UP FOR US. EPH. 5:2

"YOU WILL CALL UPON ME AND COME AND PRAY TO ME, AND I WILL
LISTEN TO YOU. YOU WILL SEEK ME AND FIND ME WHEN YOU SEEK
ME WITH ALL YOUR HEART." JER. 29:12-13

MY SOUL FINDS REST IN GOD ALONE;
MY SALVATION COMES FROM HIM. PS. 62:1

DELIGHT YOURSELF IN THE LORD, AND HE WILL
GIVE YOU THE DESIRES OF YOUR HEART. PS. 37:4

THE LORD IS MY LIGHT AND MY SALVATION—WHOM SHALL I FEAR? THE
LORD IS THE STRONGHOLD OF MY LIFE—OF WHOM SHALL I BE AFRAID?

PS. 27:1

THE LORD HIMSELF GOES BEFORE YOU AND WILL BE WITH YOU;
HE WILL NEVER LEAVE YOU NOR FORSAKE YOU. DEUT. 31:8

GOD IS WORKING IN YOU, GIVING YOU THE DESIRE TO
OBEY HIM AND THE POWER TO DO WHAT PLEASES HIM.
PHIL. 2:13

I CAN DO EVERYTHING THROUGH CHRIST,
WHO GIVES ME STRENGTH. PHIL. 4:13

IF YOU WANT TO KNOW WHAT GOD WANTS YOU TO DO,
ASK HIM, AND HE WILL GLADLY TELL YOU. JAMES 1:5

CREATE IN ME A PURE HEART, O GOD, AND RENEW
A STEADFAST SPIRIT WITHIN ME. PS. 51:10

IF ANYONE IS IN CHRIST, HE IS A NEW CREATION;
THE OLD HAS GONE, THE NEW HAS COME! 2 COR. 5:17

CAST YOUR CARES ON THE LORD AND HE WILL SUSTAIN YOU.

PS. 55:22

THE LORD YOUR GOD IS WITH YOU, HE IS MIGHTY TO SAVE. HE WILL
TAKE GREAT DELIGHT IN YOU, HE WILL QUIET YOU WITH HIS LOVE.
ZEPH. 3:17

THE LORD IS FAITHFUL TO ALL HIS PROMISES
AND LOVING TOWARD ALL HE HAS MADE. PS. 145:13

IN YOU, O LORD, DO I PUT MY TRUST. PS. 71:1

"BE STRONG AND COURAGEOUS . . . THE LORD YOUR GOD
WILL BE WITH YOU WHEREVER YOU GO." JOSH. 1:9

DEPEND ON THE LORD IN WHATEVER YOU DO,
AND YOUR PLANS WILL SUCCEED. PROV. 16:3

SINCE WE HAVE BEEN JUSTIFIED THROUGH FAITH, WE HAVE PEACE
WITH GOD THROUGH OUR LORD JESUS CHRIST. ROM. 5:1

THE LORD IS MY ROCK, MY FORTRESS AND MY DELIVERER;
MY GOD IS MY ROCK, IN WHOM I TAKE REFUGE. PS. 18:2

"IF ANYONE WOULD COME AFTER ME, HE MUST DENY HIMSELF
AND TAKE UP HIS CROSS AND FOLLOW ME." MATT. 16:24

THE WORD OF THE LORD IS RIGHT AND TRUE;
HE IS FAITHFUL IN ALL HE DOES. PS. 33:4

THE LORD IS MY STRENGTH, MY SHIELD FROM EVERY DANGER.
I TRUST IN HIM WITH ALL MY HEART. PS. 28:7

IN HIM WE HAVE REDEMPTION THROUGH HIS BLOOD,
THE FORGIVENESS OF SINS, IN ACCORDANCE WITH
THE RICHES OF GOD'S GRACE. EPH. 1:7

I TRUST IN YOUR UNFAILING LOVE. I WILL REJOICE
BECAUSE YOU HAVE RESCUED ME. PS. 13:5

LIVE A LIFE OF LOVE, JUST AS CHRIST LOVED US
AND GAVE HIMSELF UP FOR US. EPH. 5:2

"YOU WILL CALL UPON ME AND COME AND PRAY TO ME, AND I WILL
LISTEN TO YOU. YOU WILL SEEK ME AND FIND ME WHEN YOU SEEK
ME WITH ALL YOUR HEART." JER. 29:12-13

MY SOUL FINDS REST IN GOD ALONE;
MY SALVATION COMES FROM HIM. PS. 62:1

DELIGHT YOURSELF IN THE LORD, AND HE WILL
GIVE YOU THE DESIRES OF YOUR HEART. PS. 37:4

THE LORD IS MY LIGHT AND MY SALVATION—WHOM SHALL I FEAR? THE
LORD IS THE STRONGHOLD OF MY LIFE—OF WHOM SHALL I BE AFRAID?

PS. 27:1

THE LORD HIMSELF GOES BEFORE YOU AND WILL BE WITH YOU;
HE WILL NEVER LEAVE YOU NOR FORSAKE YOU. DEUT. 31:8

GOD IS WORKING IN YOU, GIVING YOU THE DESIRE TO
OBEY HIM AND THE POWER TO DO WHAT PLEASES HIM.
PHIL. 2:13

I CAN DO EVERYTHING THROUGH CHRIST,
WHO GIVES ME STRENGTH. PHIL. 4:13

IF YOU WANT TO KNOW WHAT GOD WANTS YOU TO DO,
ASK HIM, AND HE WILL GLADLY TELL YOU. JAMES 1:5

CREATE IN ME A PURE HEART, O GOD, AND RENEW
A STEADFAST SPIRIT WITHIN ME. PS. 51:10

IF ANYONE IS IN CHRIST, HE IS A NEW CREATION;
THE OLD HAS GONE, THE NEW HAS COME! 2 COR. 5:17

CAST YOUR CARES ON THE LORD AND HE WILL SUSTAIN YOU.

PS. 55:22

THE LORD YOUR GOD IS WITH YOU, HE IS MIGHTY TO SAVE. HE WILL
TAKE GREAT DELIGHT IN YOU, HE WILL QUIET YOU WITH HIS LOVE.
ZEPH. 3:17

THE LORD IS FAITHFUL TO ALL HIS PROMISES
AND LOVING TOWARD ALL HE HAS MADE. PS. 145:13

IN YOU, O LORD, DO I PUT MY TRUST. PS. 71:1

"BE STRONG AND COURAGEOUS . . . THE LORD YOUR GOD
WILL BE WITH YOU WHEREVER YOU GO." JOSH. 1:9

DEPEND ON THE LORD IN WHATEVER YOU DO,
AND YOUR PLANS WILL SUCCEED. PROV. 16:3

SINCE WE HAVE BEEN JUSTIFIED THROUGH FAITH, WE HAVE PEACE
WITH GOD THROUGH OUR LORD JESUS CHRIST. ROM. 5:1

THE LORD IS MY ROCK, MY FORTRESS AND MY DELIVERER;
MY GOD IS MY ROCK, IN WHOM I TAKE REFUGE. PS. 18:2

"IF ANYONE WOULD COME AFTER ME, HE MUST DENY HIMSELF
AND TAKE UP HIS CROSS AND FOLLOW ME." MATT. 16:24

THE WORD OF THE LORD IS RIGHT AND TRUE;
HE IS FAITHFUL IN ALL HE DOES. PS. 33:4

THE LORD IS MY STRENGTH, MY SHIELD FROM EVERY DANGER.
I TRUST IN HIM WITH ALL MY HEART. PS. 28:7

IN HIM WE HAVE REDEMPTION THROUGH HIS BLOOD,
THE FORGIVENESS OF SINS, IN ACCORDANCE WITH
THE RICHES OF GOD'S GRACE. EPH. 1:7

I TRUST IN YOUR UNFAILING LOVE. I WILL REJOICE
BECAUSE YOU HAVE RESCUED ME. PS. 13:5

LIVE A LIFE OF LOVE, JUST AS CHRIST LOVED US
AND GAVE HIMSELF UP FOR US. EPH. 5:2

"YOU WILL CALL UPON ME AND COME AND PRAY TO ME, AND I WILL
LISTEN TO YOU. YOU WILL SEEK ME AND FIND ME WHEN YOU SEEK
ME WITH ALL YOUR HEART." JER. 29:12-13

MY SOUL FINDS REST IN GOD ALONE;
MY SALVATION COMES FROM HIM. PS. 62:1